From Brokenness to Marvelous

From Brokenness to Marvelous

Marissa Laverne Daniel

From Brokenness to Marvelous
ISBN: 978-1-7320704-6-2
All Rights Reserved.

Copyright © 2020 by Marissa Laverne Daniel

No part of this book may be reproduced or transmitted in any form or by any means, graphic, electronic, or mechanical, including photocopying, recording, taping or by any information storage or retrieval system, without the permission in writing from the author or publisher.

Unless otherwise indicated, all scripture quotations are from the King James Version of the Bible.

Published by:
Ronnie J. Wells Publishing
P.O. Box 90151
Atlanta, Georgia 30364
adonai314@yahoo.com
(678) 416-8325

Cover Art by: Phanazz Concepts
(404) 579-8019

Printed in the United States of America.
All Rights Reserved under International Copyright Law.

TABLE OF CONTENTS

Dedication 1
Synopsis 2
The Introduction 4
Chapter 1 Young broken Spirit 9
Chapter 2 It's a Different World! 13
Chapter 3 You are a HOE! 17
Chapter 4 Did I make the right decision? . . 21
Chapter 5 The Leasing Office. 31
Chapter 6 Abort or Abort Not! 37
Chapter 7 "Don't want no man that does not want you." . 41
Chapter 8 BEAUTY 49
Chapter 9 A Mother's Love 53
Chapter 10 Prayers Answered. 57
Chapter 11 The Single Life! 61
Chapter 12 You're a Rose. Now go blossom! . . 65
About the Author 68
Contact the Author 70

Marissa Laverne Daniel

Dedication
☙☙

This book is dedicated to my future daughter and son. Please learn from your mother's mistakes. Remember, you both are fearfully and wonderfully made and you both are destined for greatness. Promise me that you will remain strong, even in the midst of adversity. Love you forever and always.

From: Mom ☺

Synopsis
☙☙

To the woman or girl that's reading this:
Please forgive yourself for the bad decisions you've made. If you did not go through what you went through, you would not know what you know. All things work together for good when you are on the path to your purpose. Lift your head up and fix your crown. Regardless of what you experienced, you are still a queen and a woman of God. Never forget this. You were once broken, but now you are beautiful. Go live your marvelous life!

From a girl who was once broken, but God has now blossomed me into a Marvelous woman of God.
Marissa L. Daniel

"From Brokenness to Marvelous" is based on the life of Marissa Laverne Daniel. She was born and raised in Milwaukee, Wisconsin, who left home at the age of 19 to attend Clark Atlanta University (CAU) in Atlanta, Georgia. In this powerful book, Ms. Daniel shares the difficulties she endured in her childhood and the broken, traumatic, and devastating moments she faced in college, after college, and as a young adult.

"From Brokenness to Marvelous" will help women of all ages learn how to overcome bullying, rejection, heart break, abortion, and how to love themselves. Ms. Daniel emphasized in this book how it was nothing but God's grace and mercy that helped her blossom from a broken little girl into the marvelous, woman of God she is today. She recognized important people in her life, who she refers to as 'angels', that have helped her along her journey of self-love, as well as those people who sowed good seed into her life.

Get ready and buckle your seat belt because this small book is filled with wisdom, scriptures that can help you along your journey, life lessons, and an emotional roller coaster ride that had Ms. Daniel crying and screaming her heart out to God in the midst of so much pain, guilt, and shame. She was once broken, but now she is beautiful and to God be the Glory and Honor for that!

The Lord is close to the brokenhearted and saves those who are crushed in spirit. (Psalms 34:18)

The Introduction
ぐる

At the age of 15, I developed a habit of constantly looking at myself in the mirror every five minutes. It was not to check my makeup, fix my hair, nor to remove the last piece of salad or spinach from between my teeth, but it was to simply look at myself and wonder why I was not as pretty nor light-complected as my mother. I complimented my mother time and time again on how beautiful she was to only realize that I envied her beauty, and always wanted to look like her.

I struggled throughout my young adult life on how to embrace my beauty and to truly understand that GOD CREATED ME FEARFULLY AND WONDERFULLY MADE IN HIS IMAGE. Growing up, people, especially my peers, compared me to my mother and teased me about having big breasts. As a plus size, fully developed young lady, I was very insecure about my body image. Men would not look at me directly in my eyes, but they would simply stare at my fully developed 44G breasts and just wanted to take advantage of me.

I would often hear, "I want to know what you taste like", or "You got some big ass titties". Some were bold and asked me, "When are we going to fuck?" Time and time again my heart was broken. Just like millions of women, I saw myself falling for the same men repeatedly. One person I fell for was the cool popular ladies' man, whom I gave my virginity to at the age of 14.

He basically told me broken promises, making me believe I was the only girl he had eyes for. To my surprise, he only wanted to have sex with me because he dumped me two days later and called me out of my name, that I cried for years.

When I would see him at school or at the bus stop, he would disrespect and insult me in front of my peers. I would be so scared that I would have to say a silent prayer underneath my breath for him to go away and leave me alone.

Unfortunately for this person, who basically committed statutory rape against me, and as a warning to any man or woman that has had any type of sexual relations with a minor, this is illegal and also the bible warns in Galatians 6:7, *Be not deceived; God is not mocked: for whatsoever a man soweth, that shall he also reap.*

When I went back to school, the entire freshman class knew about what happened between us, and as a result, I lost many friends. Next, I was enticed by a gorgeous football player who earned a full scholarship to Mississippi Valley State University. He was a very attractive, muscular-built young man, with beautiful smooth skin that made my heart skip a beat every time I saw his face. To my surprise again, he never had any intention on being with me and basically used me to get what he wanted. That not only included sex, but money and free meals.

Yes, you are probably thinking that I am completely vulnerable. However, these experiences taught me that in order for me to stop comparing my beauty to others, and to stop falling for the wrong men, I needed to reevaluate myself and fall in love with God as well as with myself. I now believe and understand that the question we need to ask is, "How do we stop doing what we are doing to make changes within us to make ourselves happy?" When I look in the mirror, instead of asking God, "Why didn't you make me look more like my mom?", I simply tell myself that "I AM BEAUTIFUL AND I DESERVE THE BEST". Even on your worst days, you must encourage yourself and speak positive words over your life. You do not need to wait on your pastor or a prophet to speak over your life. You have the same power that God used in the book of Genesis, when He created the earth.

I began to see that the mind is POWERFUL. The tongue is even more POWERFUL. In the Bible, it is written that *life and death are in the power of the tongue.* What we declare and speak does manifest. It is extremely important that we monitor what comes out of our mouths and to speak words of life, joy, love, and happiness. The mind is powerful, and the enemy wants our minds. Right now, I want you to cancel the assignment of the enemy over your life and break the curses that were spoken over you! It is time to rise and live the marvelous life that God has ordained for you.

"From Brokenness to Marvelous" will not only encourage you, but this book will allow you to see how God turned my ashes into beauty. You will see how my brokenness and pain from my childhood, college, jobs, and failed relationships helped transform me into a marvelous woman of God. Learn from me! God will turn your pain into purpose. We all have a story to tell, and everyone has a testimony. To the young lady that is reading this book, please know that you are not what the enemy says you are. You are more than your pretty face, your thighs, your behind, your smile, your breasts, or your waist size. You are a Queen and we all come from royalty, because we were created in the image of our heavenly Father. Our heavenly Father does not make any mistakes.

God has a purpose for your pain, a reason for your struggle, and a gift for your faithfulness. Do not give up! The past may be gloomy and sad, but the future for you is extremely bright, full of amazing opportunities. There is a rainbow that is ready to shine over your life. Get ready. Buckle your seatbelt and take God with you as we begin to blossom from brokenness into marvelous. Tell yourself that you were once broken but now you're beautiful.

Broken Spirit: Breaking someone's spirit is often done by physical, mental, emotional or sexual abuse. When a person's spirit is broken, they often feel they are not deserving of joy, or they may have lost all hope or desire for happiness. It's a feeling of total emotional defeat.

Chapter 1

೦ಙಜಾ

Young broken Spirit

The Lord is close to the brokenhearted and saves those who are crushed in spirit. Psalms 34:18

It all started at Thomas A. Edison Middle School in Milwaukee, Wisconsin. I was so excited to attend Junior High. I was so determined to be on the honor roll and to be involved in extracurricular activities. I was thrilled to make new friends and always knew in my heart that I loved school. I was determined to be an exceptional student. I did not know, before I got on the school bus, what I was about to experience. In elementary school I felt protected. Yet, in junior high, high school, college, and life after college became a journey that I will never forget. I did not know I would experience difficult, broken moments as well as a broken spirit. However, the hand of God was over my life.

Some people say that children can be the most brutal and honest people on earth. In the classroom, my peers would often question me, "Why do you talk so proper?" "Why do you act like a white girl?" I was constantly called fake and phony, so I never had a lot of friends. I would often eat in the school cafeteria by myself. As a result of the bullying and harassment, I was involved in several fights. I would be minding my own business in the school auditorium and girls behind me would pull my hair, call me bald head, or would tease me about my weight. I would run home crying to my mom about the girls in school. Both my parents were supportive and did what they could do to protect me.

I would often hear about girls plotting to fight and jump me in the school hallways or would try to catch me off guard at the bus stop. I would cry when the boys that supposedly liked me, would take my school lunch or hit me and run, because they were afraid to express that they had a crush on me. I was always the last one chosen to be on the sports team in gym class, and I felt like I could not be myself. No one at that time accepted me for who I was. Attending school in Wisconsin was tough for me, but despite the chaos and the bullying, God helped me to graduate with honors from elementary, middle and high school, while receiving so many awards and scholarships.

Throughout my childhood, I had low self-esteem and did not believe I was good enough to be accepted by my peers. During my sophomore year in high school, I slept with a knife under my mattress, having thoughts of wanting to take my own life. My mom and I attended a church in Wisconsin for twelve years straight. Unfortunately, the young ladies in that church did not want to be associated with me, and they often teased me for being a plus-size girl. My experience at this church is something I will never forget. I was often bullied by the young ladies in this church, and some of the members made me feel bad about myself. They would speak negatively over me, my mom, and my aunt.

After they kicked us out and told us it was nothing they can do for us anymore, I witnessed my own mother cry her eyes out, as we drove from California to Wisconsin in 2005. This church left my mom and I broken, and we experienced severe church hurt. The pastor was wicked and money hungry. Now as an adult, I see that we were involved in witchcraft. The bible states in Matthew 7:15, *Beware of false prophets, which come to you in sheep's clothing, but inwardly they are ravening wolves. Beware of false prophets, who come to you.* These hurtful and traumatic experiences of being constantly bullied, harassed, and put down made me question myself. I would ask myself, "Is something wrong with me" or "Why am I so different from everyone else?" I did not understand why I was not 'good enough'.

On June 13, 2007, I graduated with honors from the Milwaukee School of Entrepreneurship (MSE). Not only that, I was MSE's 2007 "Most Outstanding Student" of the Year! I received the Perfect Attendance Award and thousands of dollars in scholarships, while on my way to Carroll College in Waukesha, Wisconsin. I was honored to be selected as the

Mistress of Ceremony for my graduation ceremony. Both of my parents, my aunt, and my grandmother, Diana Lardydell, better known as KK (rest in paradise), were all smiles that day.

However, as I was standing on stage at the podium, I saw with my own eyes how some of my classmates were snickering and talking about me. Most of them did not clap for me when they announced me as "Student of the Year." Only one student from my class congratulated me. At the end of the ceremony, my mom told me, *"Marissa, everyone is not going to be happy for you. Some people are going to be jealous and envy your success. You must pray for your enemies."* I was happy to bid farewell to Milwaukee Public Schools; however, I did not know that I had just gotten off one 'roller coaster ride' and was about to get on another one, filled with new challenges and pain. At times I felt as if I would not succeed, but God brought me to the finish line!

Chapter 2

೦೫೮೦

It's a Different World!

I knew by Christmas 2007 that I could not picture myself graduating from Carroll College in Waukesha, Wisconsin. I was not happy at all. I faced racism, was misunderstood, and literally got into multiple blowouts with so many females. I felt like I was in high school all over again. Something in me kept telling me to step out on faith, and transfer to Clark Atlanta University (CAU) in Atlanta, GA, but I was so scared.

I was scared to leave my mom, scared to think that something awful would happen to me, and scared that I would end up back in Wisconsin or Indiana. However, God has a way of sending angels into your life when you need that extra push and encouragement.

One of the 'angels', Dr. Meredith Kay Reeves, who was my former high school English teacher, always believed in me. Dr. Reeves saw something in me from the moment I walked through MSE's doors. She always called me her shining star and the daughter that she never had. When I shared with Dr. Reeves how unhappy I was at Carroll University and pondering whether to transfer to another university, she patiently listened.

I explained that I was interested in attending an HBCU (Historically Black College or University), but I was afraid to transfer. Dr. Reeves was truly a blessing and she said to me, "Don't live your life in fear. The best investment you can make is an investment in yourself. So, I found myself sitting in the lobby of a Burger King fast food restaurant, completing my application to CAU.

I assembled my recommendation letters and mailed my application package to CAU, with a prayer. So many people, including my own family members, were against me attending CAU. My peers did not think I was smart enough to get accepted. Some of my family members thought I should stay home and help my mother financially, or they believed that I would end up back home in Wisconsin. I recalled at the age of 12 when one of my relatives said these words to me, *"You're not strong or brave enough to move away from home and leave your mom."* However, I learned that God will bless you in the presence of your enemies.

Dr. Reeves drove me to the airport to continue my college journey. When I arrived at CAU, I was told that I still owed $900. I had no idea where I would get the money. I only had $300.00 in my possession. In tears, I called Dr. Reeves and she sent $900 to CAU the next day. I never forgot what certain family members said to me, but then one day, my father told me to release those harsh words from my mind and heart.

As I reflect on those years, I'll never forget the moment I received a letter announcing my acceptance into CAU. This occurred on my 19th birthday, on Sunday May 25, 2008. I remember finding a summer job in Wisconsin as I anxiously awaited moving to Atlanta, GA. I did not know what to expect. I knew I would party like most college students, but I had no idea of the lessons that I would learn over the next three years. It was by God's grace that I graduated from CAU on May 21, 2012. As I walked across the stage to receive my college degree, in my mind I saw flashbacks of my college experiences. The flashbacks were God's way of showing me that all things are possible if I believe and trust in Him.

I faced so many broken, embarrassing, and painful moments while attending CAU. It was difficult for me to attend homecoming in 2014. When I was at the tailgate party, I saw the many men I was involved with during my college years. The memories of how they mistreated me were difficult to bear. I also recalled how some of the faculty and staff made me feel bad about myself academically. It took me a very long time to forgive myself for the choices that I made in college. However, in the bible Romans 8:1 states, *there is no condemnation to them which are in Christ Jesus, who walk not after the flesh, but after the Spirit.* A beautiful woman of God (Prophetess Wanda Sampson) whispered that scripture in my ear, when I was standing at the altar, overwhelmed with guilt and shame, just shortly after graduation.

Chapter 3
ଓଃ୫ଠ

You are a HOE!

Do not give holy things to dogs. Do not throw your pearls to pigs. If you do, they might walk all over them. Then they might turn around and tear you to pieces. Matthew 7:6

In 2015, I remember crying at the altar. My Pastor Sheldon Pritchard gave me a word from the Lord. He looked at me and said out loud, "You are not a hoe." I fell to the ground, crying, because in the past my peers called me a hoe. I was disgusted with myself when I reflected on the young men whom I gave my *pearls*, my temple, my body to. I was involved with several young men at CAU and Morehouse College. I remember one particular guy I was involved with at Morehouse. I thought that I was going to marry this man. He was popular, came from a wealthy background, and was one of the ministers on the college campus.

He took me out, paid for my hair salon visits, and prepared dinner for my roommates and I. I thought I was in love. He seemed to be the perfect gentleman. To my surprise, he talked negatively about me to his friends, avoided me on campus, and literally pushed me out his room, slamming the door in my face. I ended up walking down the street on James P. Brawley Drive at 2am in the morning, crying and feeling so low about myself. Throughout my college years, I was involved with young men that would have sex with me and be so disrespectful towards me afterwards. Just imagine how I felt one day while studying in the library and my ex-boyfriend entered with his friends. He began snickering, laughing, and pointing at me. I was devastated and so embarrassed.

The men that I had been involved with spread personal information about me to their friends. It took a lot of restraint to not damage their cars or any personal property I could get my hands on. Deep down inside, I was in so much pain. I once believed that I was a whore. During my junior year of college, I was almost raped by two guys at a KAPPA party, but thankfully two women burst into the room. While pulling my dress down below my knees, I ran out the room, feeling humiliated and wrought with emotion. On more than one occasion, I was the victim of date rape.

In 2011, I remember literally running to my room, crying hysterically, because some nasty guy I was with who I *thought* gave me Chlamydia. Unfortunately, still to this day I don't even know exactly who gave it to me. When I approached the young men that I had been having sex with about the STD, they all were in denial. Some of them simply avoided me. I was so humiliated and disappointed in myself. I can't even remember the man who gave it to me. I called the Chaplin at CAU and cried over the phone. I was too embarrassed to call my mom and dad during that time. The Chaplin said to me, "Marissa, this is a warning and a sign from God. You must love yourself and stop making poor decisions before you end up catching something you can't get rid of." It was tight but it was right.

I realized that I was still heartbroken over the young man who took my virginity my freshman year in high school and dumped me two days later. I was still broken over the young men that used me and did not want anything to do with me. I was still broken that I did not accept my own beauty and still compared myself to my own mother. I was still broken over the hurtful things my peers and old roommates said to me over the years that still lingered in my mind. The 12-year-old, 14, 16 and 19-year-old Marissa was broken. Unfortunately, in my early twenties, I was damaging myself more and more. I kept asking myself, "What is wrong with me? Am I really a hoe?"

I share my experiences with you, not for your sympathy, but to warn you of the dangers that lurk on college campuses and in society. Ladies never forget what God tells us, *Do not give holy things to dogs. Do not throw your pearls to pigs. If you do, they might walk all over them. Then they might turn around and tear you to pieces.* Matthew 7:6.

Chapter 4

ೋ

Did I make the right decision?

Trust in the Lord with all your heart, lean not unto your own understanding, in all your ways remember Him and He will direct your path smooth and straight. Proverbs 3:5-6.

As a student at CAU, I would often question myself, to a point that I asked one of my dear friends in Wisconsin over the phone if I made the right decision. She would say to me, "God has you there for a reason. Don't give up! You will graduate!" When I was a student at Carroll College, I had all the money in the world. I was never broke or without money. I had a campus job. My roommates and friends were jealous because I was still getting scholarships and refund checks throughout that year.

However, during that time I wished I had put that money in a savings account. I used that money to help my mother financially and spent it on things that I did not necessarily need. When I arrived at the Clark Atlanta University's campus, I faced a harsh reality.

My dad often tells people that I received a million-dollar education. He is correct. I learned a lot of life lessons and faced a lot of reality. Every semester while I was at CAU, I always had a difficult time getting enrolled due to finances.

The long lines I stood in at the financial aid office or sneaking inside the cafeteria just to get a bite to eat was draining, embarrassing, and frustrating. For several semesters, my professors were so sweet to announce my name during roll call, even though my name wasn't on the attendance sheet because I was not officially enrolled in class.

There were nights I went to bed hungry and moments that I did not have any money, not even two pennies to my name. I would go days without washing my clothes. I would look around at all the beautiful girls in the classroom, with their hair and nails done so perfectly, and here I was wearing a nappy, curly wig. I could not even afford to buy toilet paper or paper towels. During my freshman year at CAU, my roommates would hide the toilet paper from me. I would hang out with girls who would drag me with them to the malls and shop, with their $4,000 to $5,000 dollar refund checks, while I only had $15 dollars to cover my transportation and food at the mall.

Not only did I experience going to bed hungry, but I would go out on dates with guys just to have a meal to eat for the day. Was I interested in them? Absolutely not! I just wanted a meal for the day, so I would entertain them and pretend that I liked them. Not only that, but during my junior year, I was often threatened by the financial aid office of being kicked out of school or being evicted out of my apartment. The landlord would contact my roommates for them to be witnesses to watch me get evicted. I thank God it never happened! I was stressed out and worried about my finances so much that it would take my mind off my studies. Due to the financial stress I was experiencing, I did not give 100% of my effort academically to CAU.

I could count on my hands how many friends I had at CAU. I was known as the loud, bubbly, social butterfly who was very dramatic. During my first year at CAU, I was so excited to participate in a plus size girl pageant, the "Miss Bold & Beautiful Pageant". When I was selected, I was beyond thrilled. Although I struggled financially, God blessed me with resources and sponsorships from family, friends, roommates, and even Fat Philly's Restaurant in Atlanta, GA. I represented Wisconsin very well. My father, little sister and my dad's ex-wife flew in from Gary, Indiana to surprise me. This is when I had to learn to work with people who did not necessarily like me.

Some of the women in the pageant called me out of my name, yelled at me, and looked down upon me. This was a plus size girl pageant and none of the young ladies thought I fit in. I guess in their opinion, one had to be obese to be a participant in this pageant. It was ridiculous. I was set up to be disqualified and I was extremely hurt when Miss Plus Size Georgia told me in front of my father that I was disqualified when I came out and did my evening walk. I wanted to run on stage and kick the young lady's ass that was responsible for this pageant. They all knew that my evening dress was going to disqualify me but went ahead and let me wear it because they did not want me to win. Thank God my family was there. My dad said to me, "Marissa, God has already given you a crown way before you were thought of. You are fearfully and wonderfully made, and you don't need a crown from a pageant to define you. You are the true definition of bold and beautiful." Thank you, daddy.

I also know what it feels like to be evicted and have all your belongings thrown out. I decided to stay in Atlanta during the summer of 2010. I secured a summer job at the on-campus television station. I was the reporter/anchor on CAU-TV Newsbreak and this experience led me to having my very first talk show called, "Making a Difference with Marissa", on Comcast Channel 23. One of my praise dance sisters helped me by letting me stay in her boyfriend's vacant room for the summer while they both went home for the summer.

To my surprise, his room at the Heritage Commons was not paid for. The police came, yelled at me and I had to move out quickly. I cried hysterically because I did not know where to go. The police officer talked to me like I was a criminal. The few friends I had came over to Heritage Commons and helped me move my belongings. I did not know what to do or where to go. After being thrown out of the apartment that day and trying to figure out where I was going to stay, I had to go to the studio within the hour to anchor CAU-TV Newsbreak and pretend as if nothing happened. If it wasn't for God!

Thank God for one of the young ladies on campus for allowing me to stay with her for the summer. When I called my parents, they both were concerned and worried. My mother came to Atlanta that summer to check on me and to make sure I was ok. My mentor, Dr. Reeves, also came to visit me that summer. Every semester at Clark Atlanta University, I would often ask myself, "Did I make the right decision?"

Should I have stayed at a predominately white institution and continue receiving all that money? I literally had to fight my way to that graduation stage at CAU. I had to apply *the three A's* my dad taught me when I was a child: *accept, access and adapt*. When I faced those rough and challenging moments in college, I had to wipe away the tears, and with prayer, figure out how I was going to be financially enrolled at CAU, what I was going to eat, or where I was going to stay. God always made a way for me. I had to *Accept* the situation, *Access* the situation and quickly *Adapt* to it. Again, God always made a way for me. CAU's motto, "You MUST find a way or make one", also helped me in many areas of my life.

I thank God for both of my parents. My father sacrificed and helped me so much that he worked many extra hours to make sure I had something to eat at school. I felt like I was a burden to my parents and would often cry myself to sleep. I would pray and ask God for things to become easier for me in college. Struggling financially, getting into so many arguments and fights with people, not to mention the young men I got myself involved with, catching an STD, being thrown out of the apartment I was staying in, not knowing where to go or what to do, and almost getting arrested during my senior year, was so draining and I was tired. I thought God forgot all about me, but I visualized a bright future for myself and God brought my vision for my future into manifestation.

God took a $2,500 balance that I owed CAU and turned it into a balance due of only $.25 cents. I unexpectedly received the United Negro College Fund scholarship during my sophomore year. God touched people's hearts to buy me meals, groceries, and send big care packages, full of toilet paper, soap, food, personal items and money. My psychology and religion professor gave me a scholarship and my mentor paid my balance during my freshman year. During my senior year, my advisor told me that I was not going to graduate because I was missing a class.

I was a transfer student, so when I first applied to CAU, they did not accept all my credits. I called my mother from the restroom in the building on campus. I was yelling and screaming because I was so upset. My mother did not know what to say and told me to pray. I fell to my knees in prayer, asking God to make a way for me. I wanted to graduate with the CAU Class of 2012. To my surprise, my advisor called Carroll College and got the descriptions of all the courses I had completed. CAU decided to accept more of my credits. The class I did not take early on was offered the next semester, which was my last semester at CAU. It was a freshman class, but I did not care. I took that class, did my community service, passed the class with an A, and I was finally told that I was cleared to graduate. That same day, I interviewed Monica Pearson, a prominent news anchor in Atlanta, live on my talk show. To put 'the cherry on top' of a great day, I was also told that my tuition account balance was a zero! The financial aid advisor told me to stop what I was doing and thank God. If it wasn't for God!

Did I make the right decision? It's been eight years since I graduated and now, I know that my experiences were worth it. I am stronger and my faith is more solid. I will *Trust in the Lord with all my heart lean not unto my own understanding and all my ways remember him and he will direct my path smooth and straight*, Proverbs 3:5-6.

In my young life, I learned a lot of lessons, developed some tough skin, became stronger, and witnessed the hand of God work on my behalf, over and over again. I met some extraordinary people, worked with people who did not like me, and met my true best friend/sister. It was rough and it was a struggle. On graduation day, Monday May 21, 2012, I walked across that stage at CAU, on a sunny day, with my black heels on and joyful tears streaming down my face. I ended my matriculation from Clark Atlanta University with a 3.4 GPA. If it wasn't for God!

To recap, as I walked across the stage that morning, God began to show me flashbacks in my mind. He showed me images of me standing in the long lines at the financial aid office, being thrown out of Heritage Commons. He showed me moments of when I was crying because I did not know what I was going to eat, receiving eviction letters to my front door, getting into multiple arguments and fights with my peers, and the degradation from the young men I experienced. The University's Chaplin ran up to me on stage and said, "Marissa, God is good! You are graduating!"

God turned an outstanding balance into a zero. He blessed me with opportunities to intern at WISN Channel 12 News in Milwaukee, Wisconsin, WSB TV Channel 2 Action News, FOX 5 Atlanta and WCLK Jazz Station at Clark Atlanta University. My most memorable moment at CAU was interviewing WSB's retired news anchor/reporter Monica Pearson in front of a live studio audience on my talk show called, "Making a Difference with Marissa", two months before graduation.

If it was not for God, I would have never graduated. I thank God daily for keeping me and protecting me during those rough moments, even in the midst of my sin. Thank you, God, for blessing me and making a way for me when I did not see a way. I thank you God for giving me chances after chances and allowing me to be the first one in my family to graduate from college. Thank you, God, for the angels that you placed in my life during that season. I thank you Lord for my parents. Mom and Dad, thank you for believing in me, praying for me, and helping me along my journey. Thank you both for the sacrifices you made for me. Not to mention, thank you for always sending me your last and always encouraging me.

I would like to also thank the following people: Dr. Meredith Kay Reeves, Ms. Leah Gibson, Ms. Valerie Goens, Sheena Carey, Kami Jamila, Aunt Barbara Hubbard, William Lewis, Tiffany Walker, Christina Bowden, Professor Semaj Robinson, Professor Yolanda Thompson, Mrs. Murdell McFarlin, Dajuan Poe, Perisha Gibbons, Kia Michelle, Nia Green, Kaylyn Kent, the family of Kaylyn Kent, Ms. Pamela Drake, Aunt Lorraine Lardydell, Aunt Pattie Joe, Pandora Bedford, India Lee, Zahra, Monet & Roderick, Travis, Rosalyn Reed, Simone Delahoussaye, Jessica Woods, Monique Hill, Breana Wilson, Kimberly Pitts, the family of Kimberly Pitts, Samond Jones, Sheikeya Butts, Dr. Valerie Tate Green, Ericka Darrius, Sasha Rice, Changing a Generation Church and the UNCF Scholarship Fund.

Thank you to all these angels for sowing into me, feeding me, praying with me, being a friend, opening your doors to me, and for giving me a shoulder to cry on. I love you all and thank you for being there for me. You all were angels sent to me. Most of you all went on with your lives, but I will never forget the impact you made on my life during that season. Love to you always.

Chapter 5

The Leasing Office

"Marissa, you are going to have to learn how to overcome people and work with those who don't necessarily like you or think you're not equipped for the position."
Christina Bowden

In November 2012, six months after graduating from CAU, God blessed me to work in Property Management as a Leasing Professional. For eight years straight I worked with several Property Management Companies. I never knew that the Leasing Office was going to be a place where I developed tough skin, a backbone, and a place that offered so many life lessons. I recalled in 2011, when I was a junior at CAU, my best friend told me in the cafeteria that I was going to have to learn to work with people who did not necessarily like me, people who wanted to see me fail, and people who did not believe I was worthy of my positions.

In the beginning when I started my career in Property Management, I questioned God because I did not understand how a young black female, who just graduated with her undergraduate degree in Mass Media Arts, ended up in a leasing office. However, now I see why God did it. I ask myself today if I would have been humble or grateful if I got the traffic reporter position in North Carolina that I interviewed for after graduation. Was I mentally ready at that time for my television career? Would I have been arrogant and snotty toward others? God had to humble me, and most importantly, I needed to overcome challenges that some people brought to me.

I experienced stressful work environments where women stood over me, while arguing with me and trying to intimidate me. I have been spat on, while people laughed, rather than stand up for me. Oftentimes my supervisors purposefully embarrassed me in front of my colleagues. I have been threatened with termination, my former colleagues questioned my ability to do my job, and I was often assigned to work every weekend, when my colleagues were not. On many days, I was so exhausted from working that I almost passed out in my assistant manager's office. Not to mention, I had a regional manager tell me over the phone that I did not belong in his office. On various occasions, when I reacted and expressed how I felt, they were quick to call the police on me. I trained several young ladies. It broke my heart to see all these young ladies get promoted to higher positions while I was often overlooked. Through it all, I trusted God and continued to pray.

In 2017, God blessed me with my television talk show called "Broken into Beautiful", in which I advertised it through my social media outlets. During 2018-2019, God continued to bless me with so many speaking engagements, hosting opportunities, and even being a regular host for Atlanta Live on WATC. Both my regional and property managers were always lurking on my social media pages. My regional manager told me in my face these exact words in 2018. She said, "I understand that you now have a show, however, I want to make sure you are 100% loyal to your job and this company."

At the property management company, I would request days off 30-60 days in advance, but my requests were always denied. I would also be questioned by my managers why I needed the time off. I remember being ganged up on by all three of my managers about me requesting to have one weekend off a month. I was assigned to work endless weekends, which interfered with me hosting events. I remained 100% loyal to my job, but when my shift was over at 5 o'clock, I was then 100% loyal to myself, my show "Broken into Beautiful", and the other platforms that God blessed me with.

God has a way of communicating with us all. One way He communicates with me is through my dreams. I would often have nightmares about this particular property in Alpharetta, Georgia, where I previously worked. I never felt safe there, especially when I was working alone. I had dreams of people coming in the leasing office, physically assaulting me. I had dreams of men coming into the office when I was working alone, trying to rape me. I even had dreams of people holding me hostage with a gun to my head. Not to mention, in my dreams God would show me colleagues and managers talking bad about me behind my back.

I felt drained, disrespected, overlooked and broken by several jobs I held in Property Management. Sometimes, God has a way of closing doors in our faces to get us where He ordained us to be. On June 18, 2019, my manager literally slammed the door in my face, as if I was nothing to her. I wanted to kick down that door and slap the taste out of her mouth, especially by the way she made me feel, and the inappropriate things she said to me throughout my time working with her. This manager was my enemy.

I had constant dreams about her, which never made me feel comfortable working with her. As she slammed the door in my face, I took a step back and said to myself, "Marissa, the door is closed. You are free." I ran out of that office like my life depended on it. While sitting in my car, I cried and let it all out. I drove to the property's dumpster and threw my name badge, the brochures I had in my car, and even the company's tee shirts in the dumpster, and drove off like a runaway slave. For the first time in a long time I felt FREE! I made the decision to step out on faith and pursue my dreams. I would be up at 2am praying to God about my job and my desire to do what I love to do, full time.

I learned everything I needed to learn in Property Management. I became stronger and tougher. I do not regret anything about those experiences. God put me where I belonged. I learned that we all go through difficult experiences in life to make us stronger and to humble us. Now, I am much more humble, stronger, and grateful for where I am today. However, I will never forget what my favorite Property Manager in Roswell, Georgia said to me in 2015. "Marissa, have confidence in your abilities and confidence in yourself." I advise everyone who believes they are a child of God, never allow anyone to kick you out of your blessings.

Never give anyone POWER over you. You must be strong, and you must know who you are. These were all life lessons from the Leasing Office. Thank you, Father, for the lessons, the tough decisions I had to make, and the journey to get me to where I am today. Still to this day, I am exactly what my first Property Manager called me in 2012, A Leasing Diva!

Chapter 6

௪௫

Abort or Abort Not!!

I remember calling an old friend from Wisconsin, crying and screaming so hysterically that I scared her to death. She could not understand me, and it took her at least 15 minutes to calm me down. All I could say was, "Toya, I can't believe I killed my baby. How can God ever forgive me?" At that point, she totally understood me, reassuring me that everything is going to be okay, and that God's love is everlasting. On a day that changed my life, July 12, 2014, I made a decision that I never thought in a million years I would ever experience. Millions of women never thought that they too would ever experience aborting a child.

Although I was 25 years old, working a decent paying job, paying my bills, driving my own vehicle, and living the adult life, I knew that I was not mentally or even financially ready to have a child. On top of that, the man whom I had unprotected sex with suggested that I have an abortion. He already had two children of his own and of course, issues with his children's mother. I felt so alone. My mind was going back and forth about whether I should keep my baby boy, consider adoption, or abort my baby.

I had countless dreams of my baby running around the house, me holding my son, and being a loving mother. I cried for hours, even months, beating myself up for making such a selfish decision. I struggled day after day to forgive myself. In order for me to release my pain, I had to pray without ceasing. I was blessed to have my mother by my side, encouraging me, as I let my tears flow down my face as my pain and suffering were released. What hurt me the most was the child's father was nowhere to be found. During those five weeks of my pregnancy, he disappeared. Once I aborted our child, he resurfaced into my life. He chose not to be there for me. God revealed to me that he was a married man. During my brief relationship with him I always knew in my spirit that there was a question mark about him; however, him being a married man never crossed my mind. I felt ashamed that I was involved with a married man when I found out. I have learned that people will show you their true selves, especially when difficult and trying times surface.

During this time in my life, all I could do was cry and lean on God throughout this traumatic experience in my life. A minister in Miami said to the members of his church, "It's okay to cry, but don't cry for long." Your tears release the anger inside yourself. The hurt, guilt, and the pain must be released from your heart. Psalm 30:5 states, *Sobbing can remain through the night. But joy comes in the morning.*

During that time in my life, I was up during the late-night hours, crying hysterically, screaming out loud, and wanting to hurt myself. I was broken, distraught, sad, and angry. I would take a bath in my mother's garden tub, sit in the water, and cry myself to sleep. It got so bad because I was so angry with the father of my unborn child. I would have dreams of me stabbing him and taking his life. I knew I had to walk away from him before something deadly or dangerous took place that I would later regret.

I needed deliverance, but most importantly, I was having a hard time forgiving myself. I needed God, and He was waiting for me to come to Him. However, I was ashamed to call on God. I was embarrassed and so angry at myself. I could not sleep at night. I was constantly tossing and turning, when I knew that was God trying to get my attention. He wanted to hear from me. Even though He knew what I was going through, God still wanted to hear from His daughter.

I encourage all men and women of God to cry out to the Lord because He is there to comfort you, even in the midst of your pain. Never be ashamed to go to the throne.

From Brokenness to Marvelous

Never be ashamed to call on your heavenly Father. Please remember, this pain will only last a moment, and not for a lifetime. He will take that pain and make it into your purpose.

Chapter 7

ଔଃ

"Don't want no man that does not want you."

Laverne Lardydell

One day sitting in my car, I realized that throughout my young adult life, I was thirsty for a relationship. My mother once told me, "Marissa, the devil knows what you like." The enemy has such a sarcastic personality that he would send you the tall, muscular, dark skin, smooth, well groomed, rich man to sweep you off your feet." Ladies, you must be wise and ask God to give you the gift of discernment. My pastor told me that discernment comes when you have a strong relationship with God. We must be very selective with who we are letting in our inner circle of friends.

In 2017, my pastor gave me the opportunity to do the Prayer Room Announcements at WATC TV 57. I was ecstatic and nervous at the same time. I was back on television, and I rushed home from work to get ready for this opportunity. I was practicing in the mirror, while putting on my makeup. I just could not believe that God gave me another opportunity to do what I love to do. I was finally utilizing my Mass Media-Radio/TV/Film degree from CAU to give Him the glory. I never thought in a million years that I would do television ministry. I was excited that I was the first person there at WATC that evening to show up in the Prayer Room. I was not going to let Alpharetta or Norcross traffic cause me to arrive late. I was ready and on fire! My pastor, the cameraman, and the gentlemen from the production crew came in to give me instructions. As happy as I was, I could not keep my eyes off the gentleman who worked in production.

My dad once told me over the phone, in his fatherly voice, "Baby, don't ever lose your composure, dignity, and integrity over a man." Unfortunately, I made the mistake of getting involved with the gentleman who worked in production. When I was done reciting and doing the prayer room announcements, I sat down in my chair to answer some phone calls.

To my surprise, the gentleman found me on social media and sent me a private message. That private message turned into us texting, which turned into me visiting him at his radio station in College Park, Georgia. I was so impressed to see that he was a radio personality and had his own studio. He had a cool radio podcast. I would tune in every Saturday morning to support him. However, when I reflect on my relationship with him, I now realize that I admired him more than I liked him.

We went out on dates. At the time, I would drive from Roswell to Morrow, Georgia and spend the night with him on several occasions. We were intimate, and every time I spoke about a possible relationship, he would brush me off, yet, he did not want me to date other people. He was very controlling. I felt like I was wasting my time.

However, I really liked him, and was hoping that eventually we would be in a relationship. I noticed signs of him trying to control me, and that he was very selfish. When I expressed to him about how much I enjoy reciting the prayer announcements on Atlanta Live, he would intentionally hurt my feelings and say negative comments such as this: "Marissa, it's only .30 seconds." I would tell him about my co-workers at work touching my hair or asking me questions about my wigs. Yet, he still went on his radio podcast and publicly embarrassed me, sharing my personal business on his show.

Not to mention, one evening I invited him to my friend's rooftop party the night before her wedding. We decided to give the relationship a try and I thought this was a cool event for us to attend together as a couple. To my surprise, he stood me up, avoiding my phone calls and text messages. When I finally got in contact with him the next day, his response was, "My bad Marissa." I was pissed and embarrassed. I realized that I did not take my father's advice regarding men. Again ladies, never lose your composure or dignity over anyone.

I decided to go over the gentleman's house and confront him. When I knocked on his door, he answered with a disturbing look on his face. As we were going back and forth in our discussion, a woman was coming up the stairs. She was on her phone. When she was standing right beside me at his front door, she gave me a nasty look. When I asked her who she was, she began to giggle to herself, and walked into his small one-bedroom apartment as if she owned the place. He opened the door wide for her and politely said to me, "Go home Marissa, I will call you tomorrow so that we can talk."

I put my head down and ran to my car, crying hysterically. I was so embarrassed. I asked myself, "Why in the world did I drive two hours in traffic, just to waste my gas to come and confront a 48-year-old man that I never should have entertained in the first place?" I was disappointed in myself, but I could not drive home because I was so angry and embarrassed. I called my best friend. When I heard her voice, I could not stop the tears from falling from my face. She told me she was 15 minutes away from Morrow, Georgia and she was on the way. As I sat in my car, I saw them both, the gentlemen and the lady, coming down the steps. I was so angry that I got out of my car and approached them. The woman he was with tried to play 'security guard' and blocked me from approaching him. He just stood there, staring at me, speechless.

The woman decided to jump in her fancy car and drive off like a mad woman. I had so much rage in me from thinking about all the young men that ever took advantage and degraded me, that I screamed his name in the parking lot, pushing him so hard that he almost fell. We were both tussling with each other. I scratched his neck and broke his expensive headphones. Neighbors were coming outside watching. I even saw a few people recording this scene on their phones. I just knew the police were on the way. My friend, Christina, was calling me to figure out exactly where I was. He was begging me to go home because he saw the neighbors watching.

 He grabbed my car keys and shoes and begged me to go home. I was crying hysterically. I never felt so broken and embarrassed like this before, especially over a man. I fell to the ground because that is exactly where my self-love and self-esteem was: on the ground. Christina pulled up to the scene, got out of her car, and told the gentleman to just go away. I never saw anyone drive off so fast. It was as if he didn't care. Christina grabbed my hand and asked me in her concerned disappointed voice, "Marissa, where is your self-esteem? Where is the love that you have for yourself? Hug yourself right now!" I thank God for my best friend, Christina Bowden, because she came to my rescue before the situation went even further.

 That situation left me broken. I could not sleep that night. I was on my bloody knees at 2am crying out to God, asking Him to help me. I was heartbroken, angry, and needed God to fix me. I had not felt so broken, since the age of 14, when I gave my virginity to my boyfriend, who dumped me two days later. I was constantly giving my body, my time, and my energy to men who used me, degraded me, and controlled me. I felt like a toy, and I did not feel worthy enough to have higher standards. A prophet gave me a prophetic word just weeks before this incident happened. He told me that I did not know my worth. He said God does not make mistakes and that I am beautiful!

Ladies and gentlemen, please stop trying to market yourself to someone who does not understand your value! Never let a man tell you more than once that he does not want you. Please know your worth and love yourself to the point that you are okay with being alone, until God releases the man of God for you. I would rather be with myself than to deal with foolishness and disrespect. In the words of my pastor, "We don't have time to waste." Learn from your mistakes and avoid people that come into your life that will try to control, use, or hinder your growth. Never go back to anything or anyone that left you broken.

Three years later, God showed me in my dream what could have happened if Christina never showed up that evening. God took me back to that moment in the parking lot. I had on the same dress I wore that night, with the same hairstyle. I was in the same vehicle (2016 Chrysler 200) I was driving at the time. I saw myself driving on the highway heading home, crying hysterically. I got into a severe accident with a semi-truck. I crashed and was on the ground in shock, screaming, and crying for help. My nose was broken, and blood was everywhere. God saved me from a nightmare that evening! I prayed that night.

Dear God,

Thank you for your grace and mercy. Thank you for saving me and blocking the hand of the enemy. "No weapon formed against me shall prosper, Isaiah 54:17." Lord, I give you praises, and I thank you God for saving me from tragedy and events that could have harmed and killed me. I thank you Father for your hand that is over my life. Lord, I thank you that the assignment of the enemy has been cancelled. In Jesus' Name. Amen.

From: Your Daughter

Chapter 8

෬෩

BEAUTY

You created the deepest parts of my being. You put me together inside my mother's body. How you made me is fearfully and wonderfully made. I praise you for that. What you have done is wonderful. I know that very well.
Psalms 139:13-14

An old friend said to me in 2014, these exact words, *"You have always been jealous of my beauty."* I was shocked! This was someone I had been friends with since high school. This was someone that I would stop doing what I was doing to be there for her, whenever she called me. Yes, she is a beautiful woman, but I knew in my heart I was not jealous of her. At that moment I literally ran inside my walk-in closet and cried my eyes out.

From Brokenness to Marvelous

When I was in my closet crying my eyes out hysterically, an old friend from college called me to see how I was doing. He noticed that I was crying. He was concerned and asked me what was wrong. I shared with him what my friend said to me. His response was, *"Marissa, that individual is not your friend."*

The enemy has a way of speaking through people, especially the ones we are close to. My old friend put me down to make herself feel good. When I got off the phone from my friend who was encouraging me, I got up from out of my closet, looked myself in the mirror, and told myself out loud that I'm beautiful just the way I am, and I'm comfortable in my own skin. I love my curves, my thickness, my natural thick hair, and my dramatic, loud, bubbly, outgoing personality. I had to look in the mirror and fall in love with myself, and to start the process of embracing my own beauty.

I was surrounded by young ladies throughout my childhood, and through my young adult life, who thought they were better than me. The young ladies from the church I used to attend in Wisconsin, my peers from school, strangers, and old boyfriends would tease me about my body frame and my personality. I would hear people say, *"Marissa is fat. The only thing she got on her is some big ass titties. She is fake and phony. No one wants her. She is ugly. She talks too much. She is bald headed. She is way too dramatic. She is stuck up and conceited. She talks like a white girl."*

I was constantly hearing these words from people who

were bold enough to say it to my face. I began to believe the lies of the enemy. I began to believe that I was overweight, I wasn't attractive, I was bald headed, and that no man would want me. When my old friend told me in her snotty voice that I was jealous of her beauty, I cried and started comparing myself to her. It's like the enemy wanted me to be jealous of her. I had to put an end to this. I began to cry out to God, and He took me to my favorite scriptures in Psalm 139:13-15, *You created the deepest parts of my being. You put me together inside my mother's body. How you made me is amazing and wonderful. I praise you for that. What you have done is wonderful. I know that very well. None of my bones were hidden from you when you made me inside my mother's body. That place was as dark as the deepest parts of the earth.*

In 2014, I confided in a gentleman at my job about my negative experiences with men and women. He said to me, "Marissa, the reason why you were bullied, picked on, teased, and mistreated is because they saw the light in you and your peers are intimidated by that light. Don't let what others did to you crush your bubbly spirit. God was and will always be with you." Thank you, heavenly Father, that these young ladies, men, former colleagues, and old jobs are no longer in my life!

I'm Free and I'm Winning!

MARVELOUS: SUPERB; EXCELLENT; GREAT; A MARVELOUS SHOW. SUCH AS TO CAUSE WONDER; ADMIRATION, OR ASTONISHMENT; SURPRISING; EXTRAORDINARY.

For you are great and do marvelous deeds; you alone are God. Teach me your way, LORD, that I may rely on your faithfulness; give me an undivided heart, that I may fear your name. I will praise you, Lord my God, with all my heart; I will glorify your name forever. -Psalm 86:10-13

Chapter 9

ଓଃ୫ଠ

A Mother's Love

"A mother's love is the most powerful force on earth."
Catherine Keating

My mother, Laverne Lardydell, moved to Atlanta, Georgia on July 5, 2014. At the time I was 25 years old, pregnant, and I was so afraid. When she saw me, she said I looked different, and she saw a glow. At the time I was heartbroken, angry, and I felt alone. I had been used and taken advantage of by men, while still holding on to situations and events that occurred at CAU. I was being mistreated and taken advantage of at my job. I felt hopeless, and at the time, I had suicidal thoughts. When I saw my mom get out of that big truck, I wanted to run to her and hold on to her, because I realized that I needed my mother. I'm tearing up right now as I am typing this because I was broken. I did not realize how much I needed my mother's love. I needed someone here with me. The Lord sent my mother down here, and I saw my life change for the better.

When God brought my mother to Georgia, old friends faded away. The men I were involved with disappeared. My mother helped my self-esteem grow. My mother pointed out the young ladies who were my friends and the young ladies that used me. We built a special bond. I did not have anyone, including family members, trying to interfere with our relationship. This has been the best experience I had with my mother, compared to me growing up in Wisconsin.

God restored our relationship. My mother brought so much favor with her when she came to Atlanta. I started excelling on my job. I was nominated as Leasing Professional of the Year in the state of Georgia in 2017. I saw my life change for the better. I saw that I was much happier and was no longer being promiscuous or feeling low about myself. I slowly stopped comparing myself to others and started to embrace my journey. I started to finally love myself. My mom helped me to blossom into the woman I am today. She told me to be myself and to let my light shine from within. She reminded me of how beautiful I am, and she told me to cancel the negative comments that I allowed people over the years to put in my head. I was back to being jolly and bubbly. My mom helped me, not only financially, but she helped me to see the beauty inside of me. She helped me blossom from a broken little girl into a *marvelous* woman of God.

    We went shopping, had mother and daughter dates, and went out to dinner. She would have me laughing so hard, whether in the house or out in public. My mom helped me so much, and I felt *marvelous* for the first time! What a difference and such an impact my mother made on my life. I could had committed suicide, been in jail, or in a mental hospital, but God sent an angel to help me along my journey, especially here in Atlanta, Georgia. The assignment of the enemy was to use men and people to destroy me, but I thank God that assignment was canceled, in Jesus' name. Thank you, mom, for everything!

Chapter 10

☙❦

Prayers Answered

Rejection is sometimes for your protection. When I did not get the Traffic Reporter Position in North Carolina in 2012, or the CNN position that I qualified for, or the reporter/production position in Macon, Georgia that I knew I qualified for, it left me heartbroken and I felt like a failure. Not to mention, I worked hard for a position both at FOX 5 Atlanta and WSB TV. FOX told me I did not show enough initiative. The human resources personnel confused me with another intern at FOX 5. WSB picked the Caucasian woman from UGA who was barely there throughout the internship. As an intern for WSB in 2012, I made sure I was there four to sometimes six days out of the week.

It was difficult because I did not have a vehicle at the time. They would call me at 5am to come and help in the newsroom, even if it was pouring down raining outside. Regardless of the weather conditions, I still went to my job. I was very disappointed when, at the end of my internship, I was overlooked for the News Trainee position. I would be so angry to a point that when I was at home, I would sometimes throw my pillows and teddy bears at the television screen when I would see certain reporters anchoring the news.

I once thought that I was going to be a Leasing Professional for the rest of my life. It was not until my mother told me, one morning in December 2016, as she was walking fiercely on the treadmill, that I was more than a Leasing Professional. I believed at one point in my life that maybe pursuing television was not for me. After all, I was in speech class from kindergarten to the seventh grade. My kindergarten teacher told my mom that I was going to have a difficult time speaking in front of an audience.

I endured so much backlash from people, especially from my peers and staff at CAU. They were constantly tearing me down and critiquing me on my presentation, the way I talked, or how I annunciated my words. My spiritual mother, Apostle Sandra Broughton, gave me a word in 2014, that God was going to bless me with my own television talk show. It will be a show that would be centered on ministry, and one that will encourage women. She declared that the show would be sponsored, and I was going to do well. This was also confirmation from my Pastor Sheldon Pritchard. Not to mention, I would have constant dreams of me hosting a show and interviewing thousands of people on a national stage. God was speaking to me and told me that it shall come to pass in His timing.

Eight months of consistently reciting the Prayer Room Announcements for Atlanta Live, while at the same time, representing my church home, Beyond the Veil Ministries, I made up my mind to pursue my own television show. I did not care how much it would cost, or the sacrifices that I had to make. I was determined to invest in myself, so I stepped out on faith to pursue my dream. God gave me the title of "Broken into Beautiful." I experienced so many broken, traumatic, heart breaking, embarrassing moments. I have witnessed with my own eyes how God blossomed me from a broken little girl into a marvelous woman of God. I am not perfect, and I know He is still working on me. However, I have evolved, and I am not the same young lady I was in 2012, 2014, 2016 and any years afterwards.

When I wrote the vision for my show and presented it to WATC's Station Manager, he smiled at me, and congratulated me on my show idea. That was the first, "YES", I received in a long time. I literally ran outside and screamed because I was so happy. With tears of joy, I immediately called my parents. When you believe and receive the prophetic word of God, and put a demand on the word, God will blow your mind and you will see manifestation.

I dated a man who thought my 30-second prayer room announcement was nothing to be proud of. The word states, *When you are faithful over the few things, I will make you ruler over many.* God turned a .30 second announcement into a 30-minute show (Broken into Beautiful Talk Show). He then turned a 30-minute show into me hosting/co-hosting Atlanta Live, which is an hour and 30-minute live television show here in Atlanta. Not to mention, God blessed me with so many speaking and hosting engagements, and even hosting and producing a two-hour radio show on IBNX Radio Network in 2019.

Also, on Tuesday November 19, 2019, I was hired on the spot, practically immediately, to work at 104.7, The Fish Gospel Station in Atlanta, Georgia. God blessed me to go from a seasonal employee into a permanent employee. Remember, I was once rejected and turned down from so many jobs in the television and radio industry. Rejection is for your protection! My experience has been worth it, and prayers have been answered. I am in expectation of what God has up His sleeve and in His will for me. Lord, take me to the nation!

Chapter 11

The Single Life!

When asked by my colleague how long I have been single, her mouth dropped when I told her I have been happily single for five years. To my surprise, the men amongst us gave me a thumbs up. I have been single since 2015, and they have been the best years of my life. I have accomplished so much and became a stronger woman. For those of you who are single, recently divorced, or just got out of a bad relationship, this is the time to fall in love with God and accomplish those hidden desires of yours. Take advantage of this time to focus your time and energy on you and God. Here is a word of advice: "Do not be thirsty for a relationship." Being thirsty has gotten me involved in relationships that were a complete waste of my time and made me more broken on the inside.

    I used to once think there was something wrong with me, or I did not think that anyone desired me. God will block certain people from entering your life and lead you to spend time with Him. The single life for me has been a time where healing, deliverance, self-discovery, and self-love took place. Please know that you are worth the wait, so hold on to your *pearls*. One of my mentors told me a long time ago, "Marissa, everyone does not deserve a front row seat in your life." Everyone doesn't even deserve a conversation with you.

Don't be so quick to give out your phone number. I used to travel miles and miles to meet up with ex-boyfriends, and I got sick and tired of that. I felt like I was chasing them. You deserve love and you must realize your worth. I would rather be single for five years than to waste five years of my life being involved in an unhealthy relationship or chasing after men that I am not meant to be with. I am worth more than that and I am worth the wait!

Many friends of mine have gotten married, have families, or are in the process of getting engaged. The enemy wanted me to make me think something was wrong with me and for me to compare myself to them. However, I had to learn to shake that off. I had to be happy for them and celebrate them. Your time will come. You will want others to celebrate you when it's your season of companionship, love, marriage, and starting a family.

God's timing is always the best timing. I encourage you ladies and gentlemen to never lower your standards. I have been involved with men who were married, as well as men who were on the brink of a divorce and decided to go back to their wives. I was involved with men that I knew, on the inside of my spirit, that I was not ordained to be with. I made these poor decisions just to feel loved, to be wanted by the opposite sex, and to say out loud to my friends that I'm in a relationship.

When I stopped making those poor decisions, I began to embrace my singlehood and not look to the left or right. I have peace, joy, and I now have my smile back. I decided to wait for God to release the man of God He specifically created for me. I encourage you, my single sisters and brothers, to wait on God. I believe that it's going to be worth the wait for all of us. Stay strong and know that God's timing is always the best timing. All my sisters and brothers who just recently got divorced or just got released from a toxic bad relationship, please remember that there is life after a bad breakup and life after divorce. Embrace your singlehood! This is your time to heal and grow. Remember to take God with you.

Chapter 12
ಬಿತು

You're a Rose. Now go Blossom!

Ladies, it's time to rise from the pain and blossom into the women that God called for us to be. Walk like Queens and present yourself as the Virtuous Woman you are. You are a rose that may have experienced pain, suffering, abuse, neglect, criticism, but remember that God is in control and He has the final say. It's time to blossom from brokenness and overcome every fear and pain that tried to destroy you.

In order for us to blossom, we must first ask God to forgive us for our sins, and we must find the strength to forgive and love ourselves. Do not be ashamed but go to God exactly the way you are. If you have to go to God broken, bruised, confused and distraught, do not be ashamed. God can FIX it and He can FIX you. He already knows what is going on and He just wants you to come to Him and surrender.

Also, please recognize when you are broken. You know when you are hurting on the inside or when you are angry. It is imperative that you recognize the issue and go to God and ask your pastor, spiritual mother, or mentors for prayer and help during this process. Do not continue to damage yourself. If you have been raped or molested, most people do not deal with the situation during that time, especially if they are young. Sometimes people do not know what to do or who to go to. They continue to damage themselves by being promiscuous or harming others. You must seek help and cry out to God so that He can heal and deliver you. Do not be ashamed of your brokenness or your past. God can turn your pain into purpose. You are a walking testimony for someone else.

It took me a long time to forgive myself after aborting my unborn child five years ago. I had to realize that I needed to let go and move forward. If God can forgive me then I can forgive myself.

I forgive myself for the broken relationships I was involved in. I forgive myself for allowing men to take my power. I forgive myself on all the mistakes I made in my past because it helped me to become stronger and wiser. I forgive myself!

Most importantly, I forgive everyone who has ever talked about me, laughed at me, made me the butt of their jokes, used me, or cursed me. If I can forgive so can you, woman of God. Sometimes you have to be okay with a sorry you never got. The young man who took my virginity, dumped me, and who continued to disrespect and degrade me throughout my freshman, sophomore, and junior year in high school never apologized to me. I forgive him anyway and I released him to God.

> *For if you forgive men their trespasses, your heavenly Father will also forgive you. But if you do not forgive men their trespasses, neither will your Father forgive your trespasses.* Matthew 6:14-15.

During this season, fall in love with God and fall in love with yourself. You are a Rose that is ready to blossom, and I speak and declare LOVE, PROSPERITY, PEACE, JOY, GOOD HEALTH and SUCCESS in your life. Continue to walk in the favor of the Lord and allow Him to utilize you as His vessel for the kingdom. Know your worth and your value, and please know that God did not put us on this earth to be degraded. Fall in love with God and fall in love with yourself. Embrace your identity, your beauty, your gifts, and work it! Let's begin the healing process and blossom from brokenness into a marvelous testimony. Now, go live your marvelous life and carry your cross!

TAKE A LOOK IN THE MIRROR AND SMILE! God Bless!

Marvelous Marissa

About The Author

Marissa Laverne Daniel, better known as Marvelous Marissa, was born and raised in Milwaukee, Wisconsin on a sunny day on May 25, 1989. After graduating from the Milwaukee School of Entrepreneurship (2007), she attended Carroll College in Waukesha, Wisconsin. However, she always wanted to attend an HBCU (Historical Black College or University). She took a leap of faith and applied to Clark Atlanta University as a transfer student and was accepted on her 19th birthday, in May 2008. Her most memorable moment at CAU is when she interviewed WSB's TV retired news anchor/reporter Monica Pearson, in front of a live studio audience, on her talk show in college, "Making a Difference with Marissa." She graduated from Clark Atlanta University with tears of joy on May 21, 2012, with her undergraduate degree in Mass Media Arts with a concentration in Radio, TV and Film. Marvelous Marissa is on WATC TV 57, Atlanta Live monthly to encourage people to call in for prayer, and to give their lives to Christ, representing her church, Beyond the Veil Ministries. She always had a passion for television. One of her heart desires was to be a Television Talk Show Host. Through constant prayer and her faithfulness to God, He answered her prayer and blessed her with her own television talk show, "Broken into Beautiful" that airs on WATC every Sunday night at 9pm on Comcast Channel 24. She is also a regular host for Atlanta Live on WATC.

Marvelous Marissa was the first gospel radio host for IBNX Radio Network. She hosted "The Praise in You" gospel radio show, every Sunday from 3pm-5pm on NX 109 Thee Solid Rock, on IBNX radio.com. The "Praise in You" radio show was voted one of the top shows on the IBNX network. Her television talk show, "Broken into Beautiful", has become such an inspiration that she was awarded the "2018 Power Award" from the 2018 Girl Power 3 NOW Conference. She was also recognized by her Alma Mata as a "Distinguished Alumni" from Clark Atlanta University.

Marvelous Marissa is often booked for speaking engagements and hosting opportunities. She is known for her positive, and bubbly, energy that captivates the audience. Her goal is to bring smiles and laughter to the crowd. She lives by her favorite scripture, *Trust in the Lord with all your heart, Lean not unto your own understanding. In all your ways remember Him and He shall direct your path smooth and straight*, Proverbs 2:5-7.

Contact The Author

☙❧

To contact the author:
Marissa Laverne Daniel
Phone: (414) 544-3706
Website: www.brokenintobeautiful.live
Email: brokenintobeautiful17@gmail.com

www.ingramcontent.com/pod-product-compliance
Lightning Source LLC
Chambersburg PA
CBHW071031080526
44587CB00015B/2571